Burns

ISBN: 978-1-951979-87-4
Library of Congress: 2025951455
Published by Sundress Publications
www.sundresspublications.com

Book Editor: Alexa White
Managing Editor: Krista Cox
Editorial Assistant: Kanika Lawton
Editorial Interns: Elizabeth DiGrande and Ana Mourant

Colophon: This book is set in Cactus Classic Serif

Cover Image: "Blazing Prickle" by Sadee Bee

Cover Design: Kristin Camille Ton

Book Design: Alexa White

Burns

SG Huerta

Acknowledgments

Muchísimas gracias to the following venues and anthologies for publishing early versions of the following poems:

Áte Mais: Latinx Futurisms (Deep Vellum, 2024): "ignorant american"

Cobra Milk: "Phone Tag" and "Some Issues"

december: "When the group counselor talks about cortisol" and "When the group counselor calls us superheroes"

DEAR Poetry: "I Know"

en*gendered: "When your grieving anthem becomes your transitioning anthem"

FERAL and *Mid/South Sonnets* (Belle Point Press, 2023): "Texan Sonnet for a Historic Freeze" (published as "A Semi Sonnet for a Texas Snowstorm")

Garden Party Collective: "AGAINST DYING"

Ghost City Review: "I Hardly Knew My Dad Before He Died by Suicide"

Gordon Square Review: "After Staring in the Mirror Too Long" (published as "The Dorm Room Sign I Stole When I Was 18 Shows Up in Every Bathroom Selfie")

Hear Us Out! Multilingual Poems on Being Young and Growing Up in the United States - "My Phone Alerts Me About Queen Elizabeth II's Platinum Jubilee" (published as "Twitter alerts me as Queen Elizabeth II celebrates historic Platinum Jubilee")

Honey Literary: "Puberty II"

Infrarrealista Review: "Hurtless"

Lavender Review: "My Dad Calls Me a Lesbian" (published as "Poem in Which I Remember My Dad Bullying Me for Being a Lesbian")

Moss Puppy Magazine / The Minison Project: "I think I was the gayest person"

Neologism Poetry Journal: "So Much Want" (published as "Sonnet in Which the Poet's Heart Wants Out")

new words {press}: "13 Ways of Taking Testosterone"

Olney Magazine: "Texan Sonnet (I am planning a lesson on Sappho)" (published as "happy pride to everyone except cops, racists, terfs, landlords, the texas government and people who like cops, racists, terfs, landlords and/or the texas government")

Raspa Magazine's Houston City Hall exhibit *Aquí and Now:* "latinxpoética" (published as "Latinx Poetry")

smoke and mold: "Texan Sonnet (texas not just desert & cowboys but)"

South Florida Poetry Journal's JUST SAY GAY folio: "So On & So Forth" (published as "Mortality, Gender, and Other Anxieties That Are Not Unique to Me")

Split Lip Magazine: "trans poetica"

The Hellebore: "I Love Everything Inside This Mug of Coffee"

The Offing: "Named"

VIBE's anthropoetics: "anthropoetica" (published as "san martian anthropoetics")

Table of Contents

★

★★

"Everything I am
comes from a place of dying"
Joshua Jennifer Espinoza

"The earth is my home and there is
much to cry about"
Oliver Baez Bendorf

Puberty II

I never wanted any of this:
        girlhood daddy issues
more blood than I can handle
        my first period at age 10
I woke up on my dad's couch
        blood on my thighs
too scared to wake him
        I called my mom
a hundred miles away
        ended up with my dad
in the feminine hygiene aisle
        foreign to us both and grabbed
the first and least-pink thing I saw.
        This was not the only time
I hid blood from my father
        his wife found small cuts
poorly hidden by my black hoodie
        on a triple-digit summer day.
Nothing came of any of this.
        In high school I pierced every
bit of skin that wouldn't scream
        at the touch of the needles
given to me by a friend's older sister's
        older friend
by college the piercings closed up
blood didn't make me
        squirm anymore. Humbling now
to hear my voice crack
        a decade late lather T-gel on fading

shoulder cuts like my
      life depends on it. My life depends on it.
Friends are married or getting there
      while I find acne in places new to me
and recover from my first love
      weighing the cost of losing my tits
while I pick at scarred flesh.

latinxpoética

They say, *Please only send poems about the Latinx experience.*

Pero what does that mean!

I am xicanx when I conjugate poorly, tell Welita that I *used to* grade
papers when I mean I *will* grade papers después de mi cafecito.
I am xicanx whether or not the stereotypes fit.
I am xicanx when I sit down to write a poem.
I am xicanx when my favorite person brings home Takis y Jarritos de
cada sabor as a treat.

Every poem is a Latinx poem.
Every poem is a trans poem.
Every poem is a queer poem.

The first man to take notice of my potential,
pay attention to me for longer than a month,
doesn't like my poems
my gender
my hair
my first language.

My early poems were so earnest
so malleable
so reserved
so neat little left-justified lines
sad imitations of sad cishet white dudes.

19

My poems are still so earnest.   But I prefer my codeswitching pocha way of messing up/with two white supremacist colonizing languages.   I prefer the little moments that my brown &/or trans siblings &/or lovers live in.

4am

My mind has a bigger, worse
mind of its own.

So Much Want

After Cloud Delfina Cardona's "Pisces Heart"

Taking in the H-E-B flower stands,
red roses, sunflowers—what are seasons?
I'm trying to be in my body, hands
stained purple, hair dyed just to feel a burn.
I check my phone & it says rain, says my
neck & face will bleed lavender. My heart
will not stop pumping plum blood all throughout
my exhausted existence. God help me
find life outside of the floral section, out
of Lubbock, out of Texas, out of walls
packed with nature cut, processed, & packaged
just how we want. I want life outside this
body, unwanted gift. What would be left?

trans poetica

signs you might be trans:

> you only ever got in your dad's pool wearing a baggy t-shirt
> and his old red swim trunks, drawstrings tied as tight
> as possible

> you told Professor Rowan you were a boy in *Pokémon Pearl* in
> 2007

> your period serves two purposes: progressing the plot[1], and
> reminding you of what you'll ~~never~~ always have

> you're unrecognizable in high school without your new
> Modern Baseball hoodie or your yellow cardigan, the
> one that matches your dad's, layered over a slew of
> band tees stolen from your brother

> you wish you were trans, you think you might be trans, you're
> sure everyone wants to be trans[2]

> you choose the character with short black hair[3] in *Pokémon
> Shining Pearl* in 2021

---

[1] whose plot? Who knows
[2] everyone does not want to be trans
[3] relief! the rerelease removed the gender question

you don't feel it when part of you[4] gets caught in zippers or
        sticks out of your new and itchy boxers

you burst into tears unpacking boxes at 2am when your
        partner gifts you their old copy of *The Dangerous Book
        for Boys*

you love to hear the story of how your parents did not want to
        know your sex before your birth, the way your brother
        wanted you to be a boy and your sister wanted you to
        be a girl, the way your brother cried and cried when
        your parents brought you home in pink to a decidedly
        gender-neutral Noah's Ark-themed nursery, the way
        everyone eventually got what they wanted[5]

signs your dad might know you're trans:

he comes home from work and tells you about an
        employee who's a woman now[6]

he recruits your stepmom to help you *fit in* more at
        your new school[7], chunky blue eyeshadow
        pencils and American Eagle hand-me-downs
        populating your room

---

[4] you type/delete/retype any and every line about your literal body,
ultimately deleting the word dick every time
[5] just not in the way they wanted
[6] in less kind terms
[7] you never get it ~~white~~ right

he gets drunk and describes[8] the supposed brutality of
    gender confirming surgeries

he makes sure you know the Church's standing on
    queerness, makes sure you know you can have
    whatever thoughts and urges you want so long
    as you don't act on them

you don't act on them until his funeral

---

[8] in more sensationalized terms

So On & So Forth

Bury me in my cherry red Doc Martens. Gender is a performance &
my legs refuse to break. Bury me with an iced oat milk latte. Bury me
far away from my father. Gender is a performance & I'm stuck
backstage. Bury the cis girl I was before you bury the sort-of guy I am.
Gender is lineated poetry & I can't stop writing prosaic stanzas. Bury
me. Gender is. So on & so forth. Bury my gender? Is that anything?
Tell me it is (I am) something.

Mi tía texts me

only links to articles about latine poets
on cnn or the dallas morning news,
silent acknowledgment of my non-lawyer
career choices. mi tía texts me that my dad
loves me in his own way. mi tía habla con mi
mamá en español in front of mis primos
as if we are children, as if my vocabulary
is limited in both of our languages.
mi tía says nothing when a primo's presence
triggers, studies at the silverware when i yell
at my mom, no one here loves me. mi tía
guilts me over the phone when i stop
showing up, when i leave dallas and
that older cousin who got into my bed
when i was asleep. i imagine my family
texting me to be more fair to my tía in this poem.
i am certain my tía will never read this poem.

phone tag

my mom of all people had been avoiding
my calls all day & when *she* finally called
me i picked up during the opening notes
of the bojack horseman theme song *hey*—
[name redacted for transgender reasons for dead-
name reasons for [spoiler alert] dead things
to come reasons] *i'm sorry* she said

    & at that point i knew someone had died
    & she said *it's about your dad*
    & i said *did he do it himself*
    & i knew he had finally—

when my alive family made it to town someone
bought me vegan wings & an oreo shake & as i bit
into the artificial meat i thought surely this meal
is ruined surely every meal is ruined surely mi corazón
will follow every time my brain freezes

Texan Sonnet for a Historic Freeze

I should step outside, lose myself in the
snow-covered parking lot, walk to
the grocery store across the street and
keep walking, my fog of breath proof
I'm alive. It is the first Ash Wednesday
I have an excuse for not kneeling in a pew,
but my mortality is still in the room
with me. The lights and water turn on, off,
mostly off. Others have it worse.
What choices do I have? Do I water my cat
or make more pasta during rare moments
of power? Do I leave the land of state violence
in the name of Christ? Or stay and destroy
myself. The doorknob is frozen shut.

Hurtless

At 21 I had lived too long. Going through motions. Throwing half-folded t-shirts depicting artists I love more than myself into random drawers while my dad's funeral program burns holes clean through the mint recipe box my old roommate left behind. Someday this will hurt less.

I was 6 weeks away from my quince when my dad let me start stretching my ears. We thought gauges were so cool. 4 weeks in I woke up at 4am to find blood smeared all across the side of my face, my pillow. My ear lobe lost blood for hours. The hurt was worth it.

At 10, my dad announced he was leaving. Brown boxes, mostly books, populated the dining room. In his new wife's house, I helped him unpack everything from Hesiod to Reagan to Saint Thomas Aquinas to Keats, and I was not yet old enough to know our barely-existent relationship was not changing much, not really. Not old enough to know someday this should hurt less.

Yesterday I crafted a new writing playlist because Slaughter Beach, Dog keeps releasing music at the same time as my Major Life Events. Jake sings about death dead dads girls smokingpotabovehim andwatchinghellraiserontv in the song my dad told me was sacrilegious and I sing along, I sing along to my cat, to a picture of that dead man, to my neighbors through my studio's thin walls until my throat and the lyrics hurt, like I want them to hurt.

I was 19 years 7 months 10 days old the last time my dad attempted suicide without succeeding. My trauma is dripping onto the page, but the details of my life do not exist the details are not real only real in

the world of the poem it happened to the speaker of the poem they
are me but mostly not me not me not me. Someday this will hurt less.
Someday this will hurt less hurtless hurt less

Someday this will hurt less. Someday this will hurt lessurt less. Someday this will hurt less.

Someday this. will hurt less. somedaythiswillhurtless. hurt less. somedaythiswillhurtless.

Someday this will **hurt** l e s s. Someday this will hurt **lurt** l e s s. Someday this will hurt less

Someday this will hurt less. Someday this will hurt lessurt less. Someday this will hurt less.

Will this hurt less?   ill this hurt less?

Someday this will hurt less. Someday this will hurt lessurt less. Someday this will hurt less.

Will this hurt less?   **Someday this will hurt less.**   **Someday this will hurt less.**

Someday this will hurt less. Someday this will hurt lessurt less. Someday this will hurt less.

Someday this will hurt less.   Will this hurt less?   **will hurt less.**   Will this hurt less?

Someday this will hurt less. Someday this will hurt lessurt less. Someday this will hurt less.

31

My Phone Alerts Me About Queen Elizabeth II's Platinum Jubilee

Queen Elizabeth II celebrates 70 years of colonization

                                                    brutalization

                                                        theft

My dad went back to England for her Golden Jubilee
He was 32 years old in early 2002
                the year he discovered he was not an only child
                                        I am twice-removed
                                        from familia lore at
                                        best mexicanos don't
                                        talk and the english
                                        in my   family
                                        weaponize todo

In London my dad is clearly Latino
At home my dad is clearly oppressor
My dad's dad is Texas Mexican
                that is to say Huertas
                in Tejas predate anglos
                in Texas
My dad and I were invisible to each other until 2009
                        My dad's parents
        one white   one not
                myths to me until 2009
                and after that too

Shortly before his death I heard my dad talk
with my mom's mom con fluidez pero sin
acento of any sort not american ni mexicano
        pero who cares it's all lenguaje
        del colonizer y tengo la lengua
        de los dos

This is so very far from old Lizzie I am taking up space on her day
                old Lizzie
                outliving
                the only
                two English
                people I
                knew

¿What do I not know?

I can never ask or know the reasoning behind my father's
resistance to
        my quince
        that one reunión en México
        the frequent festivities y fiestas of my mother's side
        my tongue my tongue my tongue.
or when my father decided to cut his off

arte poética

Soy la luna

       pulling the tides
             letters
                  words
       out of the ocean
             mind
                colonizers' tongues—
      a matter of life
             poesía
             death
     drowning is easy
           familiar
             genetic

tengo miedo de lo que voy a encontrar en los depths

When your grieving anthem becomes your
transitioning anthem
"I'll feel better. I'll feel better. I'll feel better. I'll feel better."
—*The Front Bottoms*

If it wasn't for the changes,
    I would probably die
            before anyone saw me

how I'm supposed to be.
        I do not hate the woman
                I was; I simply traded

PINK Soft & Dreamy for Old Spice
        Wolfthorn, misogyny for transphobia.
                Maybe I should dress up

my language, my wounds. I want to pass
        as trans, wear my transness
                on a harness that digs

into my expanding waistline, wear it in my
        voice that's sure to break
                soon. Every song escaping

my cracked phone's speaker
        is a trans song, actually. Every
                poem I penned pre-pandemic

features Alive Father and his
        Cis Daughter. *I would probably*
                die.

I Hardly Knew My Dad Before He Died by Suicide

but I know he hated fireworks.

    Six Flags Fiesta Texas is popping them off

        the eve of his funeral. He's not yet able to roll

    over in his grave. Does PTSD go with you?

Frozen by loud sounds, footsteps from behind,

    men. Am I projecting? I hope it all sheds in Purgatory.

        I hope it's silenced through prayer, not

    a cold six- or twelve-pack. Prayer

hasn't brought him back, hasn't brought me

    back to the realm of the living, back to my mother

        watching but not watching the hotel TV's limited

    channels. I stand at the window for a few seconds,

the last red firework becoming past tense—

Some Issues

"And a happy ending would be slittin' my throat" —Kid Cudi

Every day I accidentally click on
one of my many bookmarked poems.

Verde que te—I have to scroll
past Logan's translation to get

to the Spanish. Sometimes I see
a picture of Lorca and share

a knowing look with him and contemplate
making fun of white folks less.

It's about coping with colonization
or something like that. Every time

I'm around family, I feel layers of gender
confidence wane and then shatter.

You don't know me, you know
my poems. (You don't know

me, you know my armchair
autopsychoanalysis.) I've lived

a lifetime I don't want my mom
to know about. She'll never ask.

Poeming is a perk of inestabilidad
mental. This shit takes persistence.

My obsessive tendencies disguise
themselves as commitment. Most

of my ink is impulse. I can't plan
for the future without getting lost

in it. One time a roommate mistook
my gender(lessness) for WomanLite,

mistook my dead-dad-depressed state
for an easy target, enveloped me in

weedhazy mornings and ginfuzzy nights
until I tried to follow my dad. Again.

Sometimes I still listen to me and my ex's
song. Sorry, it's between me and her

and the premature wedding playlist.
I hummed "Soundtrack 2 My Life"

three times before deciding on a title,
an epigraph. That most recent week

of floor-sleeping, a friend-soulmate
did a tarot reading for me. Inestabilidad

mental, the cards said. I don't remember
what cards. Pero él recuerda todo. Every year

I get scared near my birthday. *Please*. I can't get old.

Dying young(er) would've saved my dad
from hurting
            all those women. His kids,

even.

First Kill

I don't know the difference between mania
and happiness. My stability hinges on 5mg
of Abilify daily. There are so many flies

at this coffee house and I think
they're an omen of my next
bout of bipolarisms. *Save your money*

for therapy the woman behind me
tells her companion. Stranger,
I am trying, too. I am teetering

on the edge of my sanity,
swatting flies away from my face.
I keep writing about bugs, avoiding

the dead elephant in the room
and other cliches. *Save your money.*
My Abilify is free with insurance.

I need reassurance that I can grieve
any flies I kill with my own
negligence, blood and guts on my arm,

a mark where I was once markless.
With my inattention, I am a killer.
I killed my father.

On Supposedly Becoming a Woman

In a dream, I'm dancing with my father
      at the quinceañera he refuses
to pay for, a fucked up wintery
      theme, the scent of Bud Light
dancing along. He hates being
      mexicano, speaks worse Spanish
than me, his tongue stumbles over
      double r's. I know not to judge him
for this. My yellow dress billows;
      the corset slowly suffocates
the gender out of me. I am Belle from
      Beauty and the Beast,
but shorter, more mexicana and dimensional.
      He thinks I'm his daughter,
and maybe I am, but that's between us.
      Everything is relative. I don't even
know what song the quiet DJ is spinning
      as I step on my dad's feet.
I smell that Bud Light on his breath,
      always on his breath—

After Staring at the Mirror Too Long

I'm not sure what I see, not Man
or Woman, maybe a Mexican boy,
a short dyke bringing back long bangs.
Not a ton of space, but it's mine.
Too-strong cologne, vegan toothpaste,
420 dorm room sign I stole long ago,
a half-empty bottle of testosterone gel.
Sometimes I like to sit on my pink bath mat,
though it is much too small to contain me.

ignorant american

i'm an ignorant american // a lost chicana // who listens to slowed-down spanish podcasts // because i forget // how to converse // with my abuelita my friends myself, // forgetting the shape and shade // of my hands // i don't even know // the word for shoulder, // but i know the words // estereotipo and opresión // without spellcheck. // i heard // nobody calls // themselves chicana anymore. // i am nobody, // i am myself, // *yo soy joaquin,* // a politicized existence. // i'm stuck in a cliche // dreaming of the day // when i'm free // to be nobody, // inherently nothing // más que yo.

Named

I've identified more dead birds than living.
An old friend used to quiz me on flora and fauna,
pointing and asking *what's that?* but now can't see
who I've grown into, or utter the proper name. *A tree*,
I'd answer, knowing the mutability of even that. Even that.

anthropoetica

the deer here know more than i could hope to. their awareness of danger sharper.
their steps more certain. i want to know how they love. it's not a question
of if. i imagine a mother warning her fawn away from the murky
river when the sun pervades every inch of earth mid-july.
i imagine i'd be a shitty deer. i imagine my instincts
inaccurate regardless of species. i envy them.
what i'd do to stand in front of a moving
metal death trap but somehow
still survive. immortalize
me on a shitty bic
lighter from
7-11.

Sorry to the H-E-B cashier

whose express lane I zombied through
two years ago with a case of White Claw,
nail clippers, and a sheet mask sure
to leave a rash. *Self care?* she asked.
My dad just died I said, unable to stop

the words or time or my father's body
from decomposing further. *But it's fine!*
I followed up, as I so often did,
and still do. What right to sadness
do I have? What right to a dad.

On Forcing A Story That Doesn't Want To Be Told
After Eileen Myles

Last february you watched me burn a vegan grilled cheese
and you hadn't yet changed your mind about marrying me

but sometimes plans change for instance we ended up micro-
waving ramen at 2am while reading parts of *Chelsea Girls*

and taking breaks to pin more wedding ideas more
pink roses i turned on the stove fan and lit a joint

to cover the smell of my failure i read lines to you
out of context but fitting for two broke lesbian poets

just trying to make it together i tried to see the
grilled cheese not as omen but as opportunity

for growth and increased capability in the kitchen
and let me just say i want you to embrace me one

last time in this dimly lit room your shaky hands
on my waist on my insecurities because i now know

that i will not wear a navy tuxedo with rose gold
accents next year i know that those pins are now

deleted not even archived this time i know
the stupid grilled cheese was not my fault you

distracted me from the stove i'd looked away and into those
brown eyes let my guard down my 400-square-feet almost

up in flames and this has devolved into an exercise in
the power of memory i always flinch when i hear our song

but i still am here i still am

Slow Burn

Two minutes after rubbing a mud mask on my face,

it started to harden and I ran to my sink, wiped off the gray

bit by bit to reveal purple and more purple flesh, my face feeling

as if it were in front of a blow dryer on full-blast. My partner

watched me scrub and panic, calmed me, laid next to me in bed

as I closed my eyes and placed a clean wet cloth on my face.

In half sleep, I thought *is there a poem in this?* Allegory,

maybe, for how my ex said all the right things, sent the valentines

and birthday gifts, stuffed sloth with a red ribbon around his neck.

I named him Keats. Keats ended up in the dumpster with a painting

of a crooked heart I always thought looked ugly. My ex said

all the right things, until she didn't, until she became my ex

for the first, second, seventh time. The mud hardening

faster than I could react. Each time I wiped a layer off I found

myself applying more, my skin craving invisible flames.

When I came to, my partner was scrolling the internet

less than an arm's reach away, my face was cool, damp,

clear, soft. As if I'd never been burned at all.

supermercado poética
After Javier O. Huerta

Today I am going to the grocery store and I will not forget the limes
    while I compose lines in the aisles.

Last summer as I walked to the store before 8am—this detail is
    important as it was too early for this kind of thing to have
    occurred—two birds swooped down and tried to grab at my
    newly bleached hair. I suppose it's on me for trying to hide
    my mexican roots.

Mis aguacates no quieren madurar—voy a ir a la tienda pa comprar
    más.

Today I am going to the grocery store in my secondhand Adidas
    sweats and ironic t-shirt I bought for $7 from Forever 21 when
    I was 20. "What boyfriend?" it inquires, white text on H-E-B
    red fabric. I don't think lesbians were the intended consumer.
    As I peruse the plant-based milk with one headphone in, a
    woman will ask me where the hand sanitizer is but will not
    accept my response of *I don't work here*.

Today a family comes in to my part-time job, asks if we have any
    kolaches. My brain tries to process the question while my
    body nods and gestures to the case of a dozen dozens of not
    only traditional Czech kolaches but also meat-filled
    klobasneks that non-Czech white Texans call kolaches.

I used to live across the street from the best grocery store in town. To
    walk there, grab made-fresh-daily vegetarian sushi and a case
    of Lone Star, go thru the express lane, walk back to my cat

and my couch all took 10 minutes on average. Pero who's counting?

I am at the bakery today and Garry and I have the aux and we're
bumping Selena radio on my Spotify premium account I pay
for with tips and my stomach twists when older white men
with pro-cop hats walk through the door and I stifle my
reaction when someone asks for a *chuh-raw-zuh* kolache
because it takes me a moment to realize she wants *cho-ri-zo*
and I tell my coworker on register "1 chorizo!" and suddenly
soy muy self-conscious of my beaner tongue that refuses to
slow it down refuses to *chore-eez-oh* and after Garry clocks
out I feel the weight of being one of two of the bakery's
nonwhite workers.

¡Como me duele! (google docs correcting my pocha grammar)

Before we were a thing, I visited my not-yet-partner in Wisconsin,
marveled at the ability to buy liquor at Hy-Vee. That night I
got drunk on precisely 3 beers and told her that I love her,
that she should come back to Texas where H-E-B and a cute
Chicano guy lie waiting.

I am writing a poem after one of my poetic idols and about
inhabiting the weirdass space that is 21st century Chicanidad
and I am so darn frustrated by how many of the English
sentences I'm typing require me to say the subject explicitly
because english conjugates differently i have to name myself
instead of hiding in the implicit, hiding in the action.

Did you know that *beaner* has its own Wikipedia page? More links at
the bottom if you're tired of the same old slurs.

Today, I went to the grocery store for ramen & beans & tortillas & coffee creamer & I looked up from my list and saw *him*, there on an endcap: the most majestic rooster on a cloth tortilla warmer. I double checked my list—"remember: no extra shit today!"—but truth be told I always struggle to open the plastic tortilla warmer my mom got me from Fiesta.

I know a lot more words than when I decided to be a poet.

Before my dad died, I used to cook a lot more and weigh a lot less. Did you think I'd go a whole poem without mentioning my dad and his current status? I used to not be able to go a whole public outing without getting into it. (See: "Sorry to the H-E-B Cashier," a poem by a Huerta with no known relation to Javier O.)

I didn't decide to be a poet. I have a condition.

Can you believe it! I found Hub City Blend K-Cups at the store today! Tomorrow I will drink it and wonder why I thought Lubbock in a cup was a good way to start my day.

Though I was born in los estados unidos, no hablaba inglés en mis primeros años. Mi abuelita nunca aprendió como manejar (yo tampoco) y entonces fuimos al supermercado en autobús. I miss those days when I thought nothing of us being ourselves caminando y riendo, juntos, siempre juntos.

Dragonfly Elegy

You weren't supposed to die so soon.

13 Ways of Taking Testosterone

clandestine & expensive

★

the needle is all you knew existed
before the friendly misinformed nurse
told you bipolars should use topical gel
instead.

it smells like the rubbing alcohol
Welita used to rub into your scrapes
and scratches.

don't miss the delivery guy's knock
when he brings your controlled
substance.

★

sweatsweatsweatsweatsweat
sweatsweatsweatsweatsweat
sweatsweatsweatsweatsweat
sweatsweatsweatsweatsweat
sweatsweatsweatsweatsweat
sweatsweatsweatsweatsweat
sweatsweatsweatsweatsweat

★

with an estrogen supplement. seriously.
everything dry aside from the puddles
of sweat you wake up in every morning.
you are so trans, you have to trans your trans gender.

★

while pondering the lesbian-to-queer-guy pipeline

★

my mother loves me
my brother cannot see me
my sister loves me

★

is it detransition if you're too broke to continue paying? if your
friends know who you are—no, love who you are? i'm asking for
a friend.

★

out of texas, choosing survival
over home. it was never about kids.
only killing us. killing us. killing.

★

my mustache persists
to the trained eye at least

★

whether it be antidepressant or hormone therapy
i've taken to crying without shedding
tears, sobs ripping up through
my body. aching, dry
body.

★

something image heavy something metaphorical to cloak the dread i
wear like skin something positive something shiny something
masculine but not too masculine something sad for the cis readers
[erase the lines that implicate them] [erase the lines] [erase erase
erase]

★

most days
the mirror is not my enemy
anymore

★

smiling?

smiling.

I do not know how to be a good brother

even though // my first year of college I took a short-notice flight across texas // my brother was having a moment // I knew those moments in me him our dad // I drank a bottle of wine on an empty stomach the night before // blacked out // got on the plane drunk // threw up in my half sleep // wiped vomit off my leggings in the turbulence-enhanced bathroom // I did not fly for my brother but for me // my image // loving sister // I was a month away from eighteen // everything was for me

our dad is dead now // I don't know why I can't empathize // with my oldest sibling // I cannot do it unless we're crying on the ground // in the middle of a cemetery

I can't stop seeing // out of third-grader eyes // his two goldfish dead // floating // little ghosts in the too-small bowl two days after he left // for méxico he promised // a quarter a day // for kid-me to keep those fish // alive // that summer he did not leave // the proper equipment // I lied // on the phone said they were fine

I'm sorry for it now // I am // I am // selfish at heart the way our upbringing forced us to be // I only have one brother // he doesn't even know // my name

necropoetica

After torrin a. greathouse

Alcoholic veteran dies by suicide at ranch of residence in Middle of Nowhere, Texas is hardly headline-worthy these days. His absence haunts me in ways I never imagined: I consult Google for my niche theological queries & blame my bad days on a different bad man. A veces, I wish I could un-ink the memorial dragonfly from my forearm, watch it flutter & flit until it flies out of focus. Un-expand my body, un-buzz my hair until my well-maintained dyke cut regrows blacker than la noche. I wish I could hear me be a careless 21-year-old poet, drinking Fireball en la troca de mi carnal antes del art show, checking my phone for a sign of life. Go into the tall grass hiding my father's body, & find him, this time, in time.

//

Alcoholic   suicide   Nowhere
          worthy these days.   I   blame my
bad   wish I   ink the memorial dragonfly
flutter & flit   out of focus.   expand my body,   buzz
my hair   my well-maintained dyke cut   .
hear   careless   drinking   art
          a sign of life. Go into   hiding
          & find   time,   time.

//

          suicide   Nowhere
     blame my bad   body,   careless
drink   life   into   time.

The Last Great SG Poem

My date of birth and phone number
tumbled out of my mouth like questions
on this call to a new psychiatrist I snuck in
before the exterminator arrived and made
my apartment a semi-safe space once more.
When the receptionist answered I thought
I was being reverse prank called, her voice
robotic, cheerful. Exact. Too happy
for someone with my day's outcome in her hands.
I'm alive and that's supposed to be enough.
They can fit me in on Wednesday. I'm alive!
There goes $350 I can't afford not to spend.
This might be my last good poem.
I've typed up 91 poems since
my second most recent unmedicated freakout.
This doesn't count school or the drafts, ideas
populating my towering stack of journals.
It is hard to revise when I can't promise myself
tomorrow. This week has the potential to become
last March or August. I buzzed my hair last night
and I'm willing to sacrifice the red and black locks
so long as they are the only Sunday bathroom casualty.

When the group counselor talks about cortisol

I think of brown cows in fields
grazing together while alive not out

of kindness but the way the meat
tastes worse when they're stressed—

so many learned facts from my first year
of college remain: parts of a pig's

stomach, accent rules for spanish words
ending in n, what happens if you mix

a handful of pills and a handle of vodka,
the origin of the word xicana,

what really triggers, lingers, waits
in between blades of grazing grass.

When the group counselor calls us superheroes

I think *hell yeah I'm bipolar*
and I'm tired of hiding it!

My first year of college, I taught
myself: how to turn my mania into

sprawling poetry in the margins
of my Eileen Myles books,

how to eat full meals while laughing
with my best friend on the top

of a parking garage, how to pronounce
mi nombre con orgullo, resilience, resilience,

resilience!

Back

Back on meds and nauseous

                              My sister would correct me: *nauseated*

Vomiting into a pink trash can

                                    My mom would say small steps

Twenty-minute naps are now two hours

                        My partner would remind me I need the rest

Work to remember three daily pills

                               My brother would ask which ones

(At least my teeth don't grind into dust)

                    2020 me would tell 2022 me to stop complaining

Stop at two drinks maybe three

                                My late father wonders how

Living Room Still-ish Life

sleeping cat twitching cat
white and gray cat on brand new
black couch white fur black
and white cat resting on old recliner
cat too light sleeping in small sunlights
scratchy vinyl spinning circles
trembling scruffy lazy cats
two cats two humans one home
two to four homosexuals oh cat
curled up cat ear crunched against
throw pillow showstopping hiss-
scratch-sulk combo cat which cat
Halloween cat to biscuiting cat
thrifty straw-wrapper-playing cat
scratch cat's back wait come back

My Dad Calls Me a Lesbian

I once thought I was a girl
and I liked girls and I still
like girls but don't call me a girl.
Is this a poem or a confession?
Does my dad know all now,
beyond the grave? I want to write
a queer poem without his ghost
reading it over my shoulder.
I'm somewhere between girl &   other.
I was never his daughter.

Texan Sonnet

I am planning a lesson on Sappho
knowing I can get gunned down
in the middle of a fragment
or fired for the confusion of my
manwomanboygirl body or ravaged
by a virus until my brain and lungs
are once again too foggy for poems.

I finally started binding, loving it,
and it's 100 degrees in Texas. Risk:
heatstroke. Risk: dysphoria. Risk: death.
My besties are waiting at the bear bar for trivia
but I am too scared to leave my house with my body.

I don't struggle to love myself, not now.
I struggle to live in this great state.

One Flew Over

You've never been a bird-poet
or much of a formal poet, but
sometimes you see a tiny hummingbird
flitter around while you're reading Kesey
next to the unmaintained pool outside your
studio apartment and the world just stops

for you and your new ruby-throated friend.

I think I was the gayest person

at the post office
mailing out copies
of my new and tiny
and dykey zine

sitting on an IKEA
couch watching *Girls*
and trying not to
cringe at the existence
of Adam Driver

hiking at Pedernales Falls,
my cherry red boots
keeping me
from slipping off
the rocks

at my dad's funeral
last fall in my new
men's button up,
scuffed women's shoes,
saying goodbye to him
through the closed
casket and saying
goodbye as SG

in this poem
because it's my
poem and being gay
is fucking lonely a veces

catching my annual tan
at the café while
writing and drinking
a can of Lone Star,
el sol fueling
my rage and dykery

Chistosas

Welita no quería hablar when I asked her about
immigrating to this country she's *we're all* getting
older I didn't want su *nuestra* story lost she just wanted
to make jokes about papeles how easy *painful* fue–

The man behind the wheel *gringo* says
we *mexicanos* all want handouts and I cackle
when uber gives me a full refund for the ride *fear*–

My childhood best friend's dad *gringo* turned away
from la calle to face me in the backseat one day
asked if I was "an illegal" & I *stunned- wait- what-*
scared offered the texan city of my birth *pero*
a quien le importa & I told my mom years later
& in response she made a joke *bad-funny*

because if we make them laugh they'll kindly
grant us some of their humanity if we make
ourselves laugh we'll remember
we don't need them to.

(mexico)americano

con esta lengua,
soy pocha, soy
estadounidense,
soy alguien sin voz.

mi abuelita no puede oír
mis pensamientos completos
no más puedo responder con *sí* o
qué hay de nuevo o *que bueno, Welita,*
o *estoy tomando café* o *queiro decir*
algo pero no sé cómo decirlo.

me estoy de-
rritiendo
en este
olla.

(mexican)american

with this tongue,
I'm pocha, I'm
american, I'm someone
without a voice.

my abuelita can't hear
my complete thoughts.
I can only respond with *yes* or
what's new or *how nice, Welita*
or *I'm drinking coffee* or I want to say
something but I don't know how.

I'm melting
in this
pot.

Old Flame

The first cigarette was not the worst.
Sometimes I see 14-year-old me
coughing up asthmatic lungs
for the first time. I want to hug me.
I want to stamp out the still-lit cig,
send home the older boy who offered.
Stop me from stealing a pack on the patio
of D's chain-smoking parents. My growing
"rebellion" did not cause the assault.
Not everything needs to be about the assault.
I found myself watching S, one of nine
other Chicanas at school, roll us joints.
I could trust her and her neon emo band shirts
amidst the hostility. I never got caught
though I wanted to get caught. Bad.
There was never anyone around.
I see myself in college, playing adult,
how did I make it?, laughing in J's car,
hotboxing and putting away Marlboro Reds
at a Sonic Drive-In after a Chem 1 exam.
A's front yard, grass between our toes,
Crown Royal and imminent summer fling
finale between us. I stop/start/stop smoking.
So then my dad dies, right? I see myself,
third person limited, in a tiny apartment,
joining the wasps outside for my first Spirit
in months. I see me gag at the first drag.
Take another. I see two lovers, star-crossed
or bad match? I see a dead wasp twitching
on the stained concrete. I see a dead wasp.

I Need Space

Today I listened to The Cure and did
not cry for my father, for dwindling youth

and long days spent sipping Lone Star.
As a high schooler in rural central Texas,

the stars briefly filled me with wonder
while I learned to escape, dissipate,

disappear. I endured his abuse then,
and I will endure his suicide now.

Sad story. Sorry. Boys Don't Cry, right?
Those stars soon turned oppressive, vast visibility

novel and unnerving. I pictured dozens of estrellas
como la tarjeta in a game of lotería, blue and sharp

and dazzling and way out of reach. Un recuerdo:
My dad and I would sit outside and he'd talk to me

about God and the Greeks and how tiny we are
under those western constellations. I don't know

how much is posthumous fabrication,
if it was the dull, distinct smell of Bud Light

or Guinness on his breath those nights. His legacy.
All those cosmos and the persistence of cheap beer.

THERE IS NO ETHICAL LOVE POEM UNDER CAPITALISM

All lines and signs point to LOVING LESS, grind until you miss the clacking of the deer alongside your 5am walk to your third job, produce more and more until your passions are commodities and your sweat/plasma/tears pay for groceries and your trauma is an inconvenient muse, a shadowy figure always lingering next to your unmade bed.

There's no ethical consumption under capitalism, reads a mass-produced bumper sticker.

You learned to walk on the backs of your ancestors her ancestors his ancestors their ancestors your ancestors you know the soil is soaked in blood you know your two tongues are foreign to them.

All you want is love. All you want is to give the hungry man water and a small cup of coffee out of the gallons you dump out every day at closing time without losing your job.

The ship is simultaneously sinking and up in flames and you can't save anyone. You know that, don't you? So you grab a pen and turn the page, scent of coffee still on your fingers.

BUT ALL I WANT IS FOR MY BONES TO BE LOVED BY THIS EARTH

200 years of—as Ted Cruz claims—Texas Rangers keeping Texas safe.

I feel crazy reading headlines.

First day of Chicano Lit my junior year of college, the professor passed around a list of relevant people and places for the course. Half of the topics were unfamiliar. Crystal City. Texas Rangers. Others I knew. Brown Berets. United Farm Workers. He yelled at me for hablando inglés cada día but my anxiety resides in the english language. The day I learned about the massacre at Porvenir, I could not look my two white classmates in the eye.

I feel crazy in my head and in my home.

When I wake up, I swallow a pill against my throat's will, then slather 20.25mg of testosterone on my shoulders. I place a metallic star sticker on the wall calendar so everyone in the house knows my head is on straight and my gender is transed for the day.

I feel crazy remembering all the steps I have to take to make sure I don't go too crazy.

DIY HRT trends. For legal reasons, I am telling you that I am not misusing a controlled substance.

I feel crazy when I remember the Alamo.

In school, I learned how Mexicans are the enemy. In school, I learned how those Mexicans killed everyone. I learned how those damn Mexicans killed the poor, innocent settlers who started a war over the right to keep their slaves—no, I learned it was states' rights. Colonizers starting wars under the guise of independence.

I feel crazy.

I laugh at armchair archaeologists who think I care if my bones will be identified as male or female in 1000 years. Let me rest in the dirt. Come back when I care what you think.

To My Favorite Capricorn

So I'm crying in the waiting room,
accidental decaf in hand, while you enter the world.
I haven't cried in a while, but it's happening now.
I've loved you for months. Everything is changing.
My first sobrino. I want to be a good tío.
I'm scared and under-caffeinated.
But I can handle myself, I swear I can,
and god, I can't wait to meet you,
read poems to you, catch Pokémon together,
maybe even teach you guitar because your grandfather
can't. I'll be at every game, recital, birthday.
I will minimize mistakes, but I hope you'll forgive
my inevitable fuck ups, like saying bad words
to my newborn nephew, my beautiful nephew.

I Love Everything Inside This Mug of Coffee
For Miles, & after Chen Chen and Jane Wong

like the way you make it
so sweet I have no choice

but to drink it slowly, slowly,
& admire the fire of us two years in.

Nearly two years since I stopped
using cheap beer as a replacement

for psychiatry. I know sipping café
this slowly is bad for teeth but

I just want to enjoy this Modern
Baseball vinyl with you before

I have to work, want to stay
on the couch & forget Texas

wants us dead. I love us
in all our transness & queerness

& weirdness. I like to think
most Texans love us in all our

transness queerness weirdness.
Texans who know that it was

not Texas before imperialism.
This cafecito is less fuerte than

Welita makes it and sometimes
when I write poems, I see

genderless ancestors doing the same
before pen and paper. Before colonizers.

Before broken treaties. Before shame.
Before this cup of coffee.

Against Dying

Once, I vodkastumbled across my own
heart cracked open on the way to the
liquor store down the street: rubyred
shards, jagged edges, biochemical hazard.
I sank down and picked it up, fingers
pricked and bleeding bloodlessly. I don't
know what came over me; I smashed the
vulnerable thing against the asphalt over
and over and over and over until—

What I'm trying to say is,
I had to reduce myself to nothing
in order to rebecome something.
           What I'm trying to say is,
you could never outwear your welcome
on this already dying planet.
           I'm trying to tell you,
I think I understand you better than anyone ever has
or ever will. I am your blood and bipolar disorder.
I am trying to parent you, parent. I am too late.

Look. Maybe I'm not against choosing
to end the pain. I just have a big enough
guiltycatholicconscience for the both of us.

I'm telling you you flawed fatherless faltering father you poet you
person you crazy diamond to shine on—

90

I Know

You're healthier than ever / Your eyesight is 20/20 & your back does not require a single steroid shot / All those rosaries and oraciones paid off / You're drinking unlimited coffee with unlimited peppermint International Delight creamer / No one gets annoyed at the way you always leave that loud-ass fan on or use up all the Tabasco or clank your silverware against your plate while you eat / You finish every poem and essay you start and your special pens never run out of ink / You finish every home improvement project you start and everyone else in Heaven is like, Oh shit can you fix up my home too? / You aren't fucking up. / You aren't fucking up. / You aren't fucking up. / You can love, Dad. / You are loved.

Texan Sonnet

After Wanda Coleman's "American Sonnet 60" and Eileen Myles'
"Texas"

texas not just desert & cowboys but
oil to pay for college wind power
in the south plains & churches abound
stadiums & god & hurricanes displace
texans buc-ee's to save whataburger
to feed texas stars at night so big &
bright when the winter storm cuts the
lights & families pulled over on the highway
snap bluebonnet photos bits of busted
tire guns on the billboards ballots bars trucks
schools teaching texas history not really
not the story of half the state Black & brown
people made this state queer & trans people in
texas summers burning & burning & burn

Notes

The Texan Sonnet sequence was inspired by Wanda Coleman's, and Terrance Hayes' subsequent, American Sonnets.

"Texan Sonnet for a Historic Freeze" was written in the aftermath of the winter storm in 2021. Many throughout Texas were displaced or without power and other resources and our government did little to support its people.

The title of "Hurtless" was inspired by Julien Baker's "Hurt Less." The lyric quoted in the fourth stanza is from Slaughter Beach, Dog's song "Your Cat."

"My Phone Alerts Me About Queen Elizabeth II's Platinum Jubilee" was written a few months before her death. May her legacy disappear into obscurity.

"Some Issues" references William Bryant Logan's translation of Federico García Lorca's poem "Romance Sonámbulo." The poem's epigraph comes from Kid Cudi's song "Soundtrack 2 My Life."

The title of "On Forcing A Story That Doesn't Want To Be Told" is a variation of an Eileen Myles quote from their novel *Chelsea Girls*: "You can't force a story that doesn't want to be told."

"supermercado poética" was inspired by Javier O. Huerta's *American Copia: An Immigrant Epic*, a hybrid poetry collection centering around the phrase "Today I am going to the grocery store."

"13 Ways of Taking Testosterone" is after Wallace Stevens' "Thirteen Ways of Looking at a Blackbird."

The form of "necropoetica," a burning haibun, was created by torrin a. greathouse.

The title of "The Last Great SG Poem" references the Say Anything song "The Last Great Punk Rock Song."

The style of "Living Room Still-ish Life" was inspired by Say Anything's song "John McClane." The phrase "trembling scruffy lazy" in line 7 is a lyric from "John McClane."

"Against Dying" references "Shine On You Crazy Diamond," one of my dad's favorite Pink Floyd songs.

About the Author

SG Huerta is a queer Xicanx writer and organizer. They are the Poetry Editor of Abode Press, a Roots.Wounds.Words. Fellow, and Tin House alum. SG is the author of two poetry chapbooks and the nonfiction chapbook *GOOD GRIEF* (fifth wheel press 2025). Their work has appeared in *Honey Literary, The Offing, Infrarrealista Review*, and elsewhere. Find them at sghuertawriting.com, or in Tejas with their partner and cats, working towards liberation for oppressed peoples everywhere. They believe Palestine will be free from the river to the sea. They encourage you to find tangible ways to support Palestinian liberation.

Other Sundress Titles

Tales from Manila Ave.
Caoile, Patrick Joseph
$21.95

Unrivered
Vorreyer, Donna
$17.95

Death Fluorescence
Bouwsma, Julia
$20.95

Pork Fluff
Hsieh, Tiffany
$17.95

Still My Father's Son
Hikari, Nora
$17.95

The Parachutist
Hernandez Diaz, Jose
$16.00

Pure Fear, American Legend
Dzubay, Laura
$20.00

Florence
Cooley, Bess
$16.99

Spoke the Dark Matter
Whittaker, Michelle
$16.00

Back to Alabama
Smith, Valerie A.
$16.00

Good Son
Liang, Kyle
$16.00

Slaughterhouse for Old Wives' Tales
Warren, Hannah V
$16.00

D A N G E R O U S B O D I E S / A N G E R O D E S
redwood, stevie
$16.00